Self Discipline

Develop Everlasting Habits to Master Self-Control, Productivity, Mental Toughness, and a Spartan Mindset for Creating a Life of Success to Beat Addiction, Procrastination, & Laziness!

Steve Martin

Copyright © 2022 by Steve Martin - All rights reserved.

No portion of this book may be reproduced in any form without written permission from the publisher or author, except as permitted by U.S. copyright law.

Contents

Image	IV
Introduction	V
1. An Introduction To Self-Discipline	1
The Benefits of Self-Discipline	
Why Do You Want To Develop Self-Discipline?	
Living Your Life with Intent	
2. Habits	15
Break Bad Habits, Adopt Good Habits	
Self-Discipline Habits	
3. Free Goodwill	22
4. Mental Toughness	25
Visualization	
Self-Talk	
Focus	

Concentration

Mental Toughness and the US Military

5. Fear: The Destroyer of Your Persona, Self-Confidence, Self-Discipline, and Happiness … 35

 Effects of Fear on the Body

 Effects of Fear on the Mind

 Fear is Our Teacher

 A Helpful Exercise

6. Daily Self-Discipline Tips … 44

 Technique 1: Spartan Self-Discipline

 Technique 2: Navy SEAL Self-Discipline

 Everyday Tips

Final Words … 61

Image … 64

References … 65

Introduction

Some people seem to have it all. They have great jobs, flawless bodies, and beautiful marriages. They even have the energy to go to the gym in the morning! Their self-belief is unshakable. When they want to accomplish something, they just do it. They seem to most of us to be godlike.

Okay, so I exaggerated a little. Nobody has a perfect life.

Some of us get quite close. What separates these fortunate individuals from the majority? What about them attracts success after success and opportunity after opportunity? You've probably observed that these outstanding individuals have a remarkable capacity to stay optimistic and stoic, even when everything around them falls apart.

Further, have you ever wondered how people who work and live in harsh environments keep going without giving up?

Some of them seem to enjoy the task! You've surely heard of Special Ops teams that spend weeks on near-impossible missions or adventurers who spend months trekking through freezing climes.

Other extraordinary people have lifestyles that need a different kind of extreme focus and concentration. A typical day in the life of a Zen Buddhist monk, for example, consists entirely of prayer and meditation. They reject the temptations of the earthly world and devote themselves entirely to spiritual growth. They are the religious counterparts of Olympic gymnasts and Fortune 500 CEOs. How can they maintain such a high level of motivation? What motivates them?

We may answer these issues with a single word: self-discipline.

It's not really about luck, you see. Sure, some individuals are born with genes that make them more attractive or happier than the typical person. But it's their laser-sharp concentration, tenacity, and the capacity to keep going when everyone else would give up that elevates a regular Joe or Jane to superhero status. You will discover their secrets in this book.

If you've ever wondered why you never seem to live up to your full potential, this is the book for you. If you're sitting on a pile of unfulfilled goals and ambitions, get ready to change your life! You're going to discover the secret that defines every successful athlete, CEO, and performer. You'll learn how some of the world's strongest people, including Navy SEALs and Spartans, consistently confronted danger and came out on top.

Why is this issue so important to me? I didn't realize the value of self-discipline until I was in my early thirties. I'd worked for several well-known firms, succeeding in most of my responsibilities in their human resources departments. But there was always something lacking. I felt as though I were losing control of my career. After all, no matter how big my position was, my work function and knowledge level were always chosen by someone else.

My normal pattern would be: I'd apply for an exciting new job, spend the first year getting to know the business culture, but then, around the 18-month mark, I'd get a growing sensation of claustrophobia. I'd become itchy. I'd fantasize about leaving my corporate job and becoming a freelancer. What would it be like to be my own boss? But every time I attempted to visualize truly starting my own company and accepting full responsibility for my life, I ran into a brick block. I couldn't seem to make a fresh start, no matter how much I wanted to. How would I keep myself motivated to look for new clients? Who would hold me accountable for my schedule? It all felt so overwhelming. As you can expect, I was nervous. I was at a fork in the road.

What eventually tipped the scales in my favor? One discussion helped. I was sitting at the coffee shop with a considerably older coworker one morning. He'd been in his position for over ten years and he despised it. We were chatting about the holidays we were going to take that year and I admitted that for a long time I'd wanted to start my company and travel the globe, going from country to country.

He burst out laughing. "Yeah, yeah," he said. "That's something no one ever does." A rush of disgust swept over me as he went back to his desk. So this is how losing feels, I reasoned. He is correct. That's something I couldn't do. It's all a dream. I don't think I've got it in me—or do I?

I had a decision to make. I could stay where I was, talking about the same difficulties and unmet dreams year after year, or I could make a drastic shift. I had a few self-help books on hand, some of which were unopened presents.

I immersed myself in the worlds of positive psychology and self-development and discovered how to accomplish anything I want. The answer to everything? Once again, it is self-discipline.

As it turned out, I had been asking the incorrect questions all along! I had maintained the conviction that in order to be successful, I needed to be entirely confident in myself and always driven by something. I also believed that if I became "successful," my life would miraculously fall into place and I would be happy. I had a lot to learn.

After many hours of studying, thinking, and testing, today I not only manage my own HR consulting firm, but I've also documented all of my favorite discoveries and top self-discipline ideas in this book. I don't want anybody else to be stopped by a lack of self-confidence or low self-discipline anymore. I am here to help!

You can improve your self-discipline and change your life if you truly want to. I currently live a life that is better than anything I could have envisioned a decade ago and I consider myself to be very self-disciplined.

I'm not flawless. I'll reveal a few of my own flaws as we go through this book—but the younger me would be shocked at how far I've come.

This book is divided into two sections. The first section will teach you all you need to know to change your thinking from self-doubt and ambivalence to complete self-discipline. You'll discover what psychology, philosophy, and even the military have to say about motivation and what pushes us to change.

The second section goes even further, focusing on the practical tactics you can start utilizing right now to supercharge every aspect of your life. You'll learn how routines, goal-setting, and a little-known technique called the Spartan self-discipline may help you push yourself harder than ever before.

Chapter One

An Introduction To Self-Discipline

The difference between great people and everyone else is that great people create their lives actively, while everyone else is created by their lives, passively waiting to see where life takes them next. The difference between the two is the difference between living fully and just existing.

-Michael E. Gerber

JOHN GETS UP AT 5 a.m. every morning to work out. He works extremely hard at the office, ignoring distractions from his surroundings and devoting all of his attention to high-value projects. He takes a class in the evening; he will get his MBA in a few weeks.

How can people like John achieve so much consistently? And how can you achieve so much in your personal life and career? You may discover that a part of your solution is self-discipline.

There are several definitions of self-discipline. Before I outline the importance and advantages of self-discipline, I'd like you to get a piece of paper and a pen and write your own definition of self-discipline.

Compare that to my definition now that you've done it. For me, self-discipline signifies self-control, the capacity to stand out from the crowd due to distinctive habits and talents, and the elimination of everything that could end up producing bad outcomes for you.

It's no secret that the words "self" and "discipline" have an unpleasant connotation at first. In a nutshell, the two words suggest that we must "punish" or "discipline" ourselves in order to succeed. However, self-discipline is not about punishment.

Self-discipline is the capacity to control one's emotions and overcome one's flaws. It is also the capacity to pursue what one believes to be good despite temptations to abandon it. The act of self-discipline shows that one has passion and purpose (Duckworth, 2009). It demonstrates to other people that this person is prepared to do what is proper for them in terms of the outcome. It is never about what others infer; it is always about what you believe is proper or what you believe is your obligation.

The Benefits of Self-Discipline

I'm not going to lie to you. Life is difficult and it often throws you a curveball on your journey to success. This is unavoidable, but you can always do something about it and become powerful enough to tackle these problems as a professional and accomplish more than you believe you can.

With self-discipline, you can overcome these obstacles. This ability may bestow peace upon you and provide you with the tools you need to deal with any situation. It also provides you the opportunity to keep going and do whatever is in your power to achieve your goal, even if you feel like giving up.

Aside from the opportunity to rise and progress toward your goals, self-discipline is beneficial in a variety of other ways. It has a lot of advantages. Before I begin talking about them, I must tell you something else. You must understand that self-discipline is not just desirable when you are attempting to add something positive or successful to your life. This ability is also required to overcome any bad habit or addiction, such as smoking or drinking, and it is beneficial for overcoming many physical and mental health disorders (Ford, 2007).

While reading the book "The Chimp Paradox" by Dr. Steve Peters, I discovered that self-discipline offers people a basis for their character and inner strength. He made a fantastic remark that I still think about to this day. To be more precise, he emphasized in his book that you are already the person you want to be. The only thing that prevents you from realizing it is your emotional thinking. In fact, Dr. Peters claims that our emotional thoughts prevent us from behaving in the way we would prefer (Peters, 2020).

If you think about it for 60 seconds, you will understand that you are a compassionate and kind person, but that you easily lose your temper. Unfortunately, this situation will tell others that you are an angry person rather than one who is kind and caring. This does not imply that you must alter who you are to please others. All you have to do is adjust your behavior. People will see the real you this way and they will understand that you are not an angry person at all. You just have a bit of a temper. Dr. Peters used this example to help me understand the power of self-discipline. The skill enables people to better control their emotions and teaches them how to regulate their emotions as well.

Temptations, temptations, temptations. What's the matter with them? They are, in most cases, the reason why people lack self-discipline. Temptations, in fact, are the ones that throw people off course and keep them from attaining their goals (Gul & Pesendorfer, 2001). We don't understand that these temptations are just temporary, but the consequences of succumbing to them can be permanent. Self-discipline helps a lot here since it motivates people to tackle obstacles and continue on their journey. I've had a lot of problems with temptations at work. That's why I was so eager to discover a "cure." Specifically, I kept distracting myself with social media. I was constantly checking my phone, not understanding that it did not help but distract me. This gave me less time to do my work. Checking my phone was only one of the many distractions that I was facing. However, after discovering self-discipline, I understood the power of these distractions and started avoiding them. But I'll talk about myself later.

Jesse Wens once said that everyone in the world has a dream. However, in order for these dreams to come true, people must devote themselves, define themselves, and put maximum effort and self-discipline in them. This way, success is guaranteed. The third advantage of having self-discipline is a higher possibility of success. Don't get me wrong; every goal is challenging and requires sacrifice and growth. Growth does not happen overnight, yet it considerably improves your abilities, attitudes, and knowledge. Every obstacle that stands in the way of your goals may be overcome with self-discipline.

Who doesn't desire a positive relationship with their friends, family, or partner? Take out your pen and notebook once again. Now, write down what you look for in a relationship. To be more specific, what are the things that you value when it comes to your relationships with the people around you? I believe I know what you're going to write. Among others, you will most likely mention reliability, integrity, love, loyalty, and honesty. I know this since every person needs more or less the same thing when it comes to relationships. How can self-discipline assist in this situation? Self-discipline may assist you in developing better relationships by consistently displaying these character traits.

Self-disciplined people are self-assured, they can handle criticism, they always do their best, and most importantly, they never fail. In rare circumstances, if they do, they learn from their mistakes and see failure differently. It becomes an opportunity to improve themselves and become better.

Furthermore, we have been subjected to expectations and difficulties from the outside world from the day we were born. Some of our difficulties are self-inflicted, while others are imposed by other people or situations. In order to craft the life you really want to live, you must practice self-discipline.

Another important question is raised here. Do you understand why? Do you understand why you desire to develop self-discipline so much? Have you ever wondered what motivates you? Because, in order to develop self-discipline, you must first understand why you need it.

Why Do You Want To Develop Self-Discipline?

I felt like Captain America shortly after strengthening my self-discipline. This may sound like a joke, but it is real. I felt powerful enough to overcome any obstacle and pursue what I needed to live a great life and be successful. It wasn't easy in the beginning. I thought it was difficult because I hadn't learned and developed the right skills. But, as time passed, I understood the deeper issue. The issue was that I wasn't clear on why I wanted self-discipline. Yes, we all want to be better and we all want to get the skills to do that, but there is always something more than simply saying, "because I want to be better."

I sat down one day and began thinking about why I wanted this so much. My first thought was, "Because I want to be more successful in my work." Then I thought that I would love to improve my health, that I would love to stop procrastinating, that I would love to stop being distracted, that I would love to write more books, and more. Yes, I had a lot of problems that I had no clue how to fix.

You see, you need to figure out what your long-term goals are. Long-term goals are, in fact, the second takeaway of this book, apart from self-discipline. They are the motivators for you to stop being self-destructive and become disciplined.

This powerful "why" will compel you to stay on the road to success and remind you of it when confronted with a temptation. Let's imagine you wish to lose weight and get healthy. Your goals will not work if you are constantly tempted by unhealthy food. For instance, suppose someone offers you a slice of cake and you accept it. You say to yourself, *I will eat this piece of cake because one piece of cake won't harm me.* Why did you agree to take that piece of cake when you clearly said that you are on a diet? Why did this happen?

It happened because your goal isn't strong enough and it is not quite specific. In order to work toward your goals, you must first make them strong, specific, and easy to visualize. To be more precise, you must develop a powerful emotional response. Let's be a little more specific. Let's say you want to lose 20 pounds by the end of the year so you can wear your favorite dress or suit to a New Year's party. Consider how you would feel after wearing that dress or suit. How beautiful you will look and how healthy you will feel. Also, remember that you are the one in charge. You will be the one who determines what you eat and how much exercise you get each day. Now, let's go back to that slice of cake. Is it worth it to give up this wonderful vision of yourself for a piece of cake filled with sugar? Instead, eat an apple and start feeling better by remembering that you are still in control.

However, there is one element lacking from the method I just taught you. Stop for a moment and consider your "why".

Consider everything you experience at that exact moment, not just what you smell or hear. You must concentrate on it for at least 60 seconds in order to remove your attention from the temptation (Gul & Pesendorfer, 2001). Your body will return to normal after a minute of slowing down. It will not surrender to the temptation. Remember, if you make an impulsive decision when faced with a need, your choice is unlikely to be aligned with your long-term goals.

Living Your Life with Intent

I've been obsessed with intentional living from the moment I discovered it. That is because it has really improved my life. In fact, I'd love to share my story with you and assist you to better understand the concept.

You know how life is for busy people, it's always "go, go, go." I used to be like that. My existence was nothing but always being on the go. We know this condition as living "life on autopilot." I was constantly feeling like I was falling behind, yet something deep within me was telling me that I was too busy to fully be living to begin with. Looking back, this was a clear indication that I needed to take a closer look—but I didn't. Instead, I found it easier to keep living on autopilot. I made life decisions (big and small) based on what everyone else was doing and I let the momentum of those choices drag me through life.

Intentional life begins with a "why" as well. You must once again ask yourself why you want to do things, but this time you must be satisfied with the replies. Here are some questions that may help you discover your "why":

1. Why do you spend time with your friend? Why are they your friends?

2. Why did you buy something (insert what)?

3. Why did you decide to become (insert a profession)?

4. Why are you with your partner?

5. Why do you work long hours?

6. Why do you wake up late?

After you've answered these questions, consider how these responses make you feel. Are they upsetting or perplexing you? Did you find it difficult to answer some of them? Intentional living entails examining your life choices. However, it is not about obtaining all that you want at that same moment. It indicates that you have a purpose or a goal.

To explain it better, here are two examples:

1. "I am taking a creative painting class because I want to be able to reproduce one of Vincent van Gogh's paintings before I turn 40."

2. "I am taking a creative painting class because I feel inspired when I explore my creativity and I am considering painting a picture one day."

Both examples suggest intentional living. The first person has a plan, while the second person has no idea what they really want. Regardless of their different situations, one thing is clear. They live their lives intentionally. So, everything starts with your core values and vision.

Each person's core values are unique, and they are the key to selecting a proper goal. Keep in mind that every single person has different core values. For example, mine include care for my readers, care for myself, enormous amounts of self-discipline, time management, and freedom from the daily grind.

These values shape my life vision and explain my choices. So, the first step toward intentional living is defining your core values and your vision. Begin by recalling moments when you were joyful. Consider moments that made you the happiest or proudest person alive. Then start digging.

Chapter Two

Habits

CHARLES DUHIGG IS A reporter and the author of the award-winning book The Power of Habit. In it, he discusses scientific discoveries that illustrate how habits exist and how they may be changed (Duhigg, 2020). He aids us in understanding human nature and how we all have the potential to evolve.

Habits are the simple decisions we make and perform on a daily basis. They are responsible for the majority of our everyday activities. Our lives are a sum of our habits, but our habits aren't permanent. We all have some negative patterns that we follow and once we identify and break them, we make way for positive lifestyle changes. There are several strategies to change behavior, and they differ for each person. Habits are the foundation that leads to increased productivity and improved performance (Duhigg, 2020).

Break Bad Habits, Adopt Good Habits

MIT researchers illustrate how every behavior follows a neurological loop (The Massachusetts Institute of Technology, 2021). This contains three parts: a cue, a routine, and a reward. To understand your habits, you must first identify the habit loop of each of your behaviors. A feedback loop affects both positive and negative behaviors. To break negative habits or develop good habits, you must pay attention to what the loop is by employing the cue, action, and reward method.

- **Cue:** This is a trigger point that instructs your brain to go into autopilot mode and follow a set of instructions. Because we are continuously bombarded with information, identifying a cue may be challenging. Moreover, most habitual cues fall into one of the following categories: location, timing, emotional state, other people, and previous action. Assume that you eat a cookie every day, which contributes to your afternoon slump as well as weight gain. Note when you eat the cookie, what time you eat it, how you feel when you eat it, who else is around, and what you were doing right before you ate the cookie. This will assist you in isolating the cue that leads to the yearning. Are you seeking a diversion or is hunger driving your decision? Your response will determine the method to change the behavior. The cue is also a good place to start when developing a new habit. To start a routine, you must either create a new cue or identify one that already exists. For example, if you want to include exercise into your life, your cue may be wearing your jogging shoes every day after work at 6:30 p.m. This will set off the routine.

- **Routine:** This is another action that might be emotional, physical, or mental in nature. Disrupting the routine is an effective strategy to break a habit. You might keep the cue and reward while changing the routine. For example, if you are a smoker, smoking is a routine that may be triggered by stress (cue). Breaking the behavior might be as simple as doing something else when you are stressed (such as talking to someone or chewing gum).

- **Reward:** This, according to your brain, is what makes the routine worthwhile. When attempting to break a habit, experiment with several types of rewards. Take as much time as you need to find one that works for you. Rewards are psychological and the endorphin surge that accompanies them might make the current reward more appealing, even if it has negative consequences. Consider yourself a scientist gathering data points to test various hypotheses. Every time you attempt a new reward, write down your opinions about the experience. Are you satisfied? Does your finding make you nervous? Consider the values that are essential to you while looking for a reward. This way, you find the reward that works for you.

Once you've identified your loop, you can start shifting your behavior. You may either create a better routine and prepare for the cue or you can find a good reward. It's up to you. You need a strategy in any case.

So now that we understand how habits function, let's talk about how to break harmful behaviors and establish positive ones. It's worth emphasizing that if we attempt to change all of our negative behaviors all at once, we're going to fail and we'll end up feeling even worse than we did before. It's far better to focus on one habit at a time, work on it for a while, and then move on to another (Duhigg, 2020).

1. **Identify the reward:** The key to breaking a bad habit is to first identify what kind of reward we want when we respond to a trigger. Using our earlier example of afternoon snacking as an example, are you really hungry or do you need a diversion and a break from your desk?

2. **Find an alternative behavior:** Once we've identified what reward motivates us to act on a trigger, we'll be able to better understand how to change our behavior. If the reward you're looking for is reducing hunger and you want to cut down on the number of cookies you eat, consider keeping some healthy snacks at hand. A handful of unsalted mixed nuts, carrot sticks and hummus, a boiled egg, or natural Greek yogurt with berries are some examples of better snacks. When it gets close to 3 p.m. and you're hungry, head to the kitchen as usual, but instead of a cookie, have a healthy snack. If the reward you're looking for is a diversion from your job, think about other methods to enjoy a break. You may have a brief conversation with a coworker, go outside and stroll around the block once, or make a cup of herbal tea.

3. **Practice:** The next step once you've identified the reward you're searching for is to practice and put a different behavior in place. Repeating the new habit loop over and over will eventually lead to this behavior requiring less willpower and becoming automatic.

Self-Discipline Habits

The major question is still unanswered as of yet. How can we enjoy self-discipline as a way of life, both personally and professionally, and what habits should we adopt?

We can start with the habit of commitment. Disciplined people keep their promises. When they make a decision, it's set in stone and they don't even need an accountability partner to keep them on track.

Then there's the habit of temptation avoidance. Isn't it difficult to resist temptation? So, guess what? It's difficult for everyone, even the most disciplined person. They are not always better at resisting temptation; they are just better at avoiding it altogether!

Last but least, there's the habit that makes you create new habits from time to time. Many people consider a disciplined life to be full of deprivation. But that's not a good way to look at it. Simply notice that you are forming a new habit, which takes time and energy to establish.

Chapter Three
Free Goodwill

PEOPLE WHO HELP OTHERS (with zero expectations) experience higher levels of fulfillment, live longer and make more money. I'd like to give you the opportunity to convey this value during your reading or listening experience. In order to do so, I have a simple question for you...

<u>Would you help someone you have never met if it did not cost you money, but you did not get credit for it?</u>

If so, I have a 'request' to make on behalf of someone you do not know. And probably never will. They are just like you, or like you were a few years ago: less experienced, full of desire to help the world, looking for information but unsure where to look....this is where you come in.

The only way for me, to accomplish my mission of helping other people is, first, by reaching them. And indeed, most people judge a book by its cover (and reviews). If you have found this book valuable so far, would you please take a brief moment right now and leave an honest review of the book and its contents? It will not cost you a dollar and less than 60 seconds.

Your review will help....
....one more person to find a way to improve their life.
....one more individual support his or her family.

....one more friend experiencing a change they would never have experienced otherwise.

....one more life change for the better.

To make that happen...all you have to do is....and this takes less than 60 seconds....leave a review.

P.S. - If you feel good about helping a faceless people, you are my kind of people. I'm really excited to helping you improve in the coming chapters (you'll love the tactics I am about to share).

P.P.S. - Life hack: if you introduce something valuable to someone, they associate that value with you. If you'd like goodwill directly from another person - send them this book.

Thank you from the bottom of my heart. And now back to our regular program.

- Your biggest fan, Steve.

Chapter Four

Mental Toughness

MENTAL TOUGHNESS IS RELATED to the study of performance psychology, and it was originally used to help elite athletes perform better. It emerged as a field of study in the mid-1980s and research continues to this day by developing mental toughness techniques and techniques to educate athletes, businesspeople, and all other types of performers to come up with breakthrough results.

The term "mental toughness" refers to the ability to persevere in the face of adversity while remaining positive and competitive. It also entails training and preparing yourself to be mentally prepared for whatever challenge comes your way (Jones, Hanton, & Connaughton, 2007).

Staying mentally strong will not only provide the strength we need to deal with our mistakes or poor performance, but it will also give us the resilience to keep going in the face of setbacks. When events don't go our way (or the way we want them to), we can't lose concentration or determination. We must continue to persevere through the adversity with which we are faced, according to the very definition of mental toughness.

Making routines, using visualization techniques, and practicing self-talk are all strategies to increase mental toughness.

Visualization

Visualization, according to top-performing athletes, is critical in maintaining and enhancing mental toughness before and during competitions (Jones, Hanton, & Connaughton, 2007). Mark Plaatjes, a marathon runner and gold medalist, accomplished everything with the help of visualization and mental toughness. It is clear from his triumph in the 1993 World Championships Marathon that he has incredible mental toughness. Plaatjes was able to take the win with just three minutes to spare by studying images of the course and using visualization techniques to imagine himself running the course several times before the race.

The power of visualization, especially in athletic training, is mind-boggling, and makes it clear how useful it can be when used correctly. Using visualization correctly is clearly subjective, as each person benefits from different techniques. What worked for Mark Plaatjes may not work for you (Jones, Hanton, & Connaughton, 2007).

Regardless of individual differences, it is always necessary to visualize positive outcomes while being realistic and expecting the unexpected (good or bad). Visualizations should be detailed and outline exactly what you intend to achieve without opportunities for errors and changes in plans.

Finally, remain confident and calm while hoping for the best, even if the chances are stacked against you. Remaining confident may seem simple, especially before a race or competition, but when the stakes are high, it is sometimes more difficult than it appears. In reality, it's quite easy to get discouraged as an athlete, especially if your performance hasn't met your expectations.

Self-Talk

Self-talk strategies have been demonstrated to increase confidence and improve mental toughness in a variety of situations, from the workplace to the court, track, or field.

Individuals may improve their performance by reframing critiques and using motivating self-talk. Developing personal affirmations (I am mentally strong), a list of achievement reminders (I won first place last time), and personal pep convos (I can do it) may increase mental toughness during lapses in self-confidence It is important to remember that self-talk is most effective when it is realistic. "I can win against this opponent because I have this pitch in my arsenal" is an example that is more effective than saying, "I will beat this person."

Focus

If you're looking for the quickest approach to unleash your potential to be mentally strong or self-disciplined, start with your capacity to concentrate. Without concentration, we are prone to deviating from anything or anybody that requires our attention. The lessons and exercises in this chapter emphasize the importance of safeguarding, expanding, and optimizing your capacity to concentrate.

One of the most significant impediments to having strong concentration is the lack of a clear sense of where you're headed. Take a minute before starting your next project to reflect on why you're doing it in the first place. Ask yourself the following questions:

1. What do I want to achieve?

2. What is my motivation for my actions?

3. Why is reading this book or this project important to me?

4. How will this project or book add meaning to my life?

When you do this exercise, you will know where you want to go and your work will proceed more smoothly. Take a few minutes to describe how things will look and feel once you've reached your goal.

Concentration

You've probably heard the phrase "I must concentrate..." We all use this once in a while, even when it comes to simple things like eating, walking, driving, writing, and more serious duties like attempting to complete a significant project. The key to success is the power of concentration. Concentration helps revive our dormant energy and channels the power inside us to ease our road to better ideas and sucess. It is also an important aspect in mental toughness and self-discipline development.

When this skill is well developed, your mind obeys you quickly and does not follow meaningless ideas. Concentration is crucial in meditation, developing mental mastery, and achieving peace of mind. Without it, the mind just bounces from one notion to another. Do you have any ideas on how to improve it?

1. **Attention:** The state of your attention reflects brain activity. Attention is directly related to concentration and learning. If your attention is scattered and fragmented on numerous things and places, your brain activity is likewise scattered and fragmented and you are unable to concentrate well and understand information easily.

2. **An Appropriate Environment:** Another crucial factor that determines concentration power is finding an appropriate environment, regardless of whether you are attempting to concentrate on your studies, employment, or any other task; the proper environment is a requirement if you want to concentrate well on your objective.

3. **Reading:** Reading is another really effective approach to improving your concentration. We're

all guilty of reading something or the other. Many of us like reading a newspaper every day and maybe more are addicted to non-fiction, fiction novels, or worse, social media. The idea is to read a couple of pages from the newspaper or a book and then take up a pen and paper and write down whatever you have gained or learned from what you read.

Mental Toughness and the US Military

Here's an excellent illustration of mental toughness. Every year, around 1,300 cadets join the United States Military Academy, located at West Point. Cadets must complete a series of brutal exams during their first summer on campus. This summer initiation program is known all over the world as "Beast Barracks."

According to researchers who have discussed with West Point cadets, "Beast Barracks is deliberately constructed to test the very boundaries of cadets' physical, emotional, and mental capacities."

You would think that cadets who successfully complete Beast Barracks are larger, stronger, or tougher than their classmates. Angela Duckworth, a researcher at the University of Pennsylvania, found something different when she started tracking the cadets.

Duckworth's research uncovered how mental toughness, perseverance, and passion impact the ability to achieve goals. She tracked a total of 2,441 first year cadets at West Point. She recorded their high school ranks, scores, leadership potential score (which indicates participation in extracurricular activities), and physical aptitude exams (a standardized physical exercise evaluation).

Here's what she discovered. It wasn't a cadet's strength, intelligence, or leadership potential that accurately indicated whether or not he would complete Beast Barracks. Instead, it was grit—the perseverance and passion to achieve long-term goals—that made the difference.

In fact, cadets with one standard deviation higher on the Grit Scale were 60% more likely than their peers to complete Beast Barracks. It was mental toughness, not talent, IQ, or genetics, that determined whether or not a cadet would be successful.

What is mental toughness for you?

Find out what mental toughness is for you. For the West Point Army cadets, mental toughness means finishing summer at Beast Barracks. For you it may be:

- One month without missing a workout
- One month without processed food
- Delivering work ahead of schedule
- Meditating every day
- Working out more than usual
- Calling a friend every Saturday
- Spending every evening doing something creative

Whatever it is, be clear about where you're heading. Mental toughness is an abstract quality, but in the real world, it is tied to concrete actions. You can't just think your way to being mentally strong; you have to prove it to yourself by accomplishing something of value to you in real life.

Chapter Five

Fear: The Destroyer of Your Persona, Self-Confidence, Self-Discipline, and Happiness

WHAT EXACTLY IS FEAR? Is it positive or negative? Why is fear important, and what, if anything, does it have to do with blind people? Fear, at its most fundamental level, is a physical and emotional reaction to some external stimulus. Sometimes the stimulus is obvious—for example, a loud, unexpected crash in the middle of the night—but the trigger for fear is subconscious and difficult to trace.

Some aspects of fear are evolutionary; they are a hardwired set of autonomic responses that have been important to our survival, according to science (Ranchman, 1990). There is debate over the number of evolutionary fears, but two are often mentioned—fear of falling and fear of loud sounds. Evolutionary fears may be the root of other fears—consider, for example, fear of heights—but there are many fears that do now show proof of being hardwired into our brains.

Have you ever heard of escape rooms? Escape rooms are rooms in which people are locked in order to play a game that requires them to solve a series of puzzles in a certain amount of time in order to complete a goal, often obtaining the key to unlock the room. What have they got to do with fear?

When creating a dangerous escape game, escape room designers take a lot of factors into account. This includes the three fundamental types of fear: primal, irrational, and rational. Knowing the differences between these three types of fear is what makes or breaks a dangerous escape room.

Fear may be really powerful. Have you noticed? It causes us to doubt our abilities, suppress our creativity, and leave our dreams unfulfilled. If you ask me, living in fear is no way to live.

I've been studying fear for years, and here's what I've learned. You can't beat it, overtake it, ignore it, support it, or deny it (Ranchman, 1990). Push fear away or pretend it doesn't exist and all you get is more of its familiar effects, limitation, confusion, and disappointment in yourself. The only long-term, intelligent method to deal with fear is to take away its power.

How do you do that? By making fear your friend.

It may seem counterintuitive, but here's how it works. Resisting fear empowers it. Unseen fear creeps into your thoughts and takes control of your body. However, giving it your full, open, loving attention takes it out of the shadows.

Once you learn to recognize how fear drives your choices, you can choose differently by letting joy, enthusiasm, wholeness, and love into your life. This is how you kill fear and learn to live your life.

Familiarize yourself with fear in all of its manifestations. Make learning a way of life. Learn to see how it clouds your judgment and convinces you that you are not your intelligent, magnificent self.

Become an expert in your fear and it will lose its power over you. Make it your friend for life and your life will begin to sing its own unique and beautiful song.

Effects of Fear on the Body

Some of us come into the world predisposed to fear. You may have tension, anxiety, and inner agitation.

Make a practice of learning these bodily sensations. You'll be able to recognize fear as it begins to take hold. Focus on the sources of your fear, which are deep within you. Don't analyze or push them away. Simply feel and breathe, feel and breathe, feel and breathe.

Understand that these are only bodily sensations. There's no need to build a story around them or let them guide your decisions. Simply note them, then move on with living your beautiful life.

Exercise, do yoga, practice deep breathing, stroll in nature, and meditate to take good care of your fear-prone body. Be a kind host, even if fear is present. Know that a place of essential wholeness is inside you that has never been touched by fear and live from there.

Effects of Fear on the Mind

Fearful thoughts revolve around the word "no." They tell us we cannot, should not, and are not capable of something. They persuade us that if we express our true heart's desire, we will be judged, rejected, or abandoned. They make our heads whirl incessantly with worry. Do any of these ring a bell?

- I can't disappoint her/him.
- I might not succeed at this.
- I have doubts about doing this.
- I might feel overwhelmed.

- I will need to work hard.
- What happens if I get heavily criticized?
- What if things get more difficult?
- I do not know how to start doing this.
- I am so scared.

These ideas weave a familiar web, leaving you frustrated and unable to change. But this is not your true voice. This is simply fear speaking.

Here's how fear works. It makes you believe that it knows what the future holds and makes you expect only negative outcomes.

What is the truth about the future? You have no idea. You have no idea whether you will succeed or fail. But your fear-fueled mind convinces you that you will fail. And if you believe these thoughts, no wonder fear will paralyze you. What if what really happens is fantastic beyond your wildest dreams? What if you let yourself remain realistic, accept that you don't know what the future holds, and let life unfold naturally?

Why go one more second believing limited thoughts with bleak outcomes that aren't even true? Here's some medication for your fear-fueled thoughts:

- Pay attention to your mind so you can understand how it functions. Learn to recognize your own fear-driven thoughts.

- Take the prudent approach. Don't trust what your thoughts are saying. Recognize what is genuinely true: you don't know what the future holds.

- Feel the liberation of being free of a bleak future that hasn't even occurred yet. Life is suddenly brimming with possibilities. Can you sense them?

Act

- You now understand how crucial it is to befriend your fear.
- You're aware of how fear manifests in your body.
- You can see how fear infiltrates your head.

This is the point at where the rubber meets the road. You have a choice. What do you really want now that you're no longer driven by fear? What do you want your life to be about?

Harness the power of fear by completely understanding it. Then locate your true voice - the one that is alive inside you and cannot be squelched no matter how much you believe in fear. When you're ready, get up and sing a note of your own wonderful song.

Fear is Our Teacher

Empowerment is the opposite of fear. Facing our fears is the most powerful method for us to learn about ourselves, develop from experience, and become a better, more empowered person. This was a core component of every young person's life in traditional societies, also known as initiation.

Ancient Europeans and many other nations lost their indigenous customs as a result of imperial invasion, which began with the Romans and continues to this day. Thankfully, there are still societies all over the globe that know that making fear a friend may result in deep change.

Fear is a bare mirror that reflects our deepest wounds, weaknesses, and shadows. However, every time you choose to face your fears, you are choosing to learn more about yourself and the world around you.

A Helpful Exercise

Instead of struggling with your ideas and stressing about whether they are good enough, make a commitment to yourself that you will no longer torture yourself. Take a deep breath and then let your thoughts and words flow. To prepare yourself for overcoming your fear, remind yourself, "I am an outstanding _____," and fill in the blank with the role you are attempting to play. For example, convince yourself, "I am an amazing writer," and then rush through the last few pages of your chapter. Repeat "I am" affirmations any time you feel the need to calm yourself.

Chapter Six

Daily Self-Discipline Tips

FOLLOWING THROUGH WITH AND completing the tasks we begin is a terrific approach to increase the potency of our self-discipline skills. When we leave a task incomplete, our minds remain in a state of tension even after we've moved on to other things to concentrate on. This phenomenon is connected with the Zeigarnik effect, named after psychologist Bluma Zeigarnik, who observed in 1927 that study participants who were given tasks and completed them performed twice as well as those who were not (Pashler, 2016).

Spending our leisure time worrying about what we haven't completed is seldom enjoyable or effective. Make it a habit to work step by step and be persistent until your task is finished. You'll discover how to avoid procrastination and fulfill your own drive to do the assignment.

Another strategy to improve our ability to complete our tasks is to get more comfortable with the concept of success. Many individuals confess to being terrified of success. To go boldly in that direction, we must perceive ourselves as worthy of achievement.

Though success often brings with it more responsibility and a heavier workload, it also enhances our capacity to deal with those changes. As you find more success, you are more driven to continue.

Your responsibility now is to hold on tight and believe that everything will be fine—and it will. You are adaptable, powerful, and resilient.

What do you do when you want to give up? This is the point in the self-discipline journey that we may choose to endure despite experiencing irritation and low energy. We can also choose to yield to the part of ourselves that doesn't feel capable enough to complete a task.

The fastest path to a happy ending here is to make it a habit to constantly encourage yourself. This habit may incorporate as many diverse tasks as you need to keep yourself focused on your objective.

It may be as simple as reminding yourself of the next actionable step, using a tracking sheet, listening to high-energy music, taking a small break, or speaking with someone who can cheer you up.

It doesn't matter how you encourage yourself so much as it does that you keep encouraging yourself. You'll leave space for procrastination if you don't put your heart into it. We can overcome procrastination and have the drive to see our endeavors through when we believe in ourselves.

First and foremost, you must prevent burnout. Burnout occurs when you are intellectually, emotionally, or physically exhausted. Burnout may occur when a constant stream of incoming demands is met without pauses or ways to eliminate stress. Burnout may occur even when we are doing something we like; in fact, burnout can occur when we begin missing meals or sleeping less in order to spend more time doing something we enjoy.

Fortunately, there are several strategies to prevent burnout. The most crucial suggestion is to build a consistent, everyday practice. Working at a steady pace prevents us from having to pull all-nighters or work under duress until the very last minute.

Another strategy to avoid burnout is to set reasonable goals for yourself. Understand that your energy, creativity, and production will have ups and downs. Avoid the need to push yourself incessantly to get things done. There's no need to fall into a productivity trap when you put in lots of effort but get nothing in return.

Always be gentle to yourself and enjoy the improvements you're making along the way.

It is critical to ensure that you have enough free time. Give yourself genuine breaks on a regular basis to maintain your mind and body in good working order. Get outside—nature can be restorative and a welcome distraction from the work you do inside.

Another strategy to keep oneself healthy while working toward your goal is to recognize that although you may fail, you can turn failure into a great learning experience. What if you learned to see failure as only a signal to choose an alternative path forward? What if you determined that failure is just something that has to be worked out, reorganized, or reassessed, rather than an indication of your own weakness or failure?

We no longer have to be terrified of failing when we consider failure as something that may occur while making progress. Failure may be seen as an opportunity to try again, as well as a circumstance that may provide solutions for future success.

When your levels of self-discipline begin to wane, it may be time to start rewarding your efforts again. After you've performed the initial task, you may add prizes for achieving milestones, which are activities or accomplishments that must be achieved to unlock the ultimate goal. This will redirect your attention and motivate you to work harder. Make incentives that are unique or fascinating to you. The benefits might be physical, such as buying a new sweater, or intangible, such as the satisfaction of sticking to your fitness regimen five days in a row. For example, you might write a list of five methods to reward yourself for continuing to make improvements.

Now, I'd like to present to you some more useful examples, strategies, and tactics for developing self-discipline.

Technique 1: Spartan Self-Discipline

The Spartans were incredibly straightforward and disciplined. Their only purpose was to become fierce warriors and maintain Lycurgus' rules. Sparta got weak and finally faded away when they let the temptation of wealth, food, and luxury slip in.

Spartans had a few rules that they always followed:

- They had a simple life.
- They were against weakness and overindulgence.
- Wealth was not a concern.
- Character, merit, and discipline were of the utmost importance.
- Warfare and fitness were everything to them.
- Long hair was seen to be masculine.
- They were people of few words.

I've always liked the saying, "Don't pray for easy lives; rather, pray to be a stronger person." Take a moment and ask yourself:

- Have you ever prayed or wished to become more powerful?
- Have you ever prayed or wished to be safe or protected?

Your answer to both questions is likely yes. Now, think about this. What if instead, you prayed regularly to become more resilient, stronger, and more disciplined? What would happen then? I know the answer. People would be thrust into situations in which they would need to be stronger, more resilient, and more disciplined. That is quite interesting. This made me rethink discipline. So I started researching it from this perspective.

The Spartan Way of Life

The Spartans were unrivaled in terms of discipline. Everything they did was motivated by a single goal: to be the best warriors possible. They excelled in just one thing, which was warfare.

They grew so focused on this that they lost sight of the necessity for anything else. Lycurgus, who is known as Sparta's father, crafted a system of rules. In this system, money was made of wood and land was split among all people, so that merit and character were valued more than money.

According to Aristotle, freedom comes with discipline. Every individual in the world desires freedom, particularly those who have permanent life responsibilities such as spouses, children, and parents and those whose jobs are devoid of meaning.

The work itself isn't always devoid of meaning. However, there are many expenses that the work is supposed to provide for, including:

- Car payments
- Mortgage payments
- Eating out
- Buying things

Those things do not provide freedom but they need to be covered. Instead, as your income grows, so do your possessions. This does not equal more freedom, however. Here's an example from the Spartans:

Once upon a time, a man (Spartans were focused on males rather than females) was astounded by how modest King Agesilaus' and all Spartans' clothes and meals were. "Freedom is what we receive from this way of life, my friend," King Agesilaus said. Discipline is built through time through the choices that a person makes; it does not begin in the womb. Consider all of the decisions you've already made today:

- The choice of waking up to the alarm or hitting the snooze button.
- The choice of eating a healthy breakfast or merely cereal or a pop tart.
- The choice to exercise or not to exercise.
- The choice to browse social media or work on a project.

Discipline may be seen as a sequence of decisions. The more proficient you grow at making decisions, the more disciplined and liberated you will become.

The Simple Spartan Discipline

Spartans were famous for their simple statements. Sparta was known as Lacedaemon, from which the term "laconic" comes.

A laconic phrase, also known as laconism, is a short or concise remark, particularly an elliptical and blunt rejoinder. It is called after Laconia, a region of Greece that includes the city of Sparta, whose ancient people were known for their linguistic austerity and for their blunt and sometimes snappy comments.

Philip II of Macedon is a noteworthy example. He shifted his attention to Sparta after capturing southern Greece and obtaining the surrender of other significant city-states. He questioned menacingly whether he should approach as a friend or adversary. "Neither," was the response. "You are urged to surrender without further delay because if I send my army into your territory, I will burn your fields, slaughter your people, and raze your city," he said, losing patience. The Spartan ephors responded once again with a single word: If. As a result, neither Philip nor his son Alexander the Great tried to take the city.

Speaking was essential in Sparta. If you did not speak up, then you were not worth it at all. This kind of terseness appeals to me and it is most noticeable in those who have a clear sense of purpose and discipline. At the end of the day, character, honesty, merit, and hard work are valued more than being well-dressed, having the latest phone, or posting the best pictures on Instagram.

Learn to talk less while doing more because:

- Doing > Talking
- Freedom > Stuff

The Spartan way of life suggests:

Simplifying your life

Spartans were indifferent to money or possessions. Instead, they were concerned with freedom, even if it meant dying for it. It was essential to preserve their laws and discipline.

Most people nowadays have no moral compass or stance. Instead, they give in to everything they fancy and bend to every whim. Mass consumption is corruptible in the same way that leprosy is. If a person is unable to abstain from what they want, they will constantly be playing a losing game.

This is terrible. If there are 12 people in a room and you put 12 cookies on the table and warn them not to eat them, a few will eat one and persuade others to eat theirs as well. In the end, there is always going to be one person that won't eat one and another one who will eat two cookies.

The person who chooses to not have one has control over themselves. Others may believe they have power, but they do not. Real power is having control over your earthly fleeting desires. Make your life easier. Get rid of what you don't need and learn to live with less.

Becoming physically fit

The Spartans were well-known for their commitment to physical fitness. After all, they were supposed to be lifetime warriors and we were forbidden from pursuing any other occupation except that of a fighter in the military.

You must be physically fit, much like the Spartans were. That way, you will learn how to become disciplined. Spartans didn't simply work out; they trained constantly.

Technique 2: Navy SEAL Self-Discipline

This elite group of soldiers is focused on achieving success in difficult and unexpected terrain. They see their suffering as a source of joy. They emphasize resilience and proficiency in order to become invincible. On the path to success, you must concentrate on aspects that might propel you to success and you must redefine yourself. Elite Navy members simplify their lives and train like Spartans did, and they also:

Don't quit

"I will not quit," states the Navy SEAL creed. "In the face of hardship, I persevere and thrive. I will get back up if I am knocked down every single time. I'm never out of a battle." There will be many problems and barriers in life. This sometimes necessitates venturing into seas that you are unfamiliar with. Persistence and dedication will propel you past these obstacles.

Pay close attention to everything they learn

Focus on your prior experiences and use them to your advantage, whether it's a mistake you've made in the past or something a mentor has taught you. Leadership is taught and learned in the Navy SEAL. To be successful in life, you must learn to make adjustments along the way. You must be versatile, move quickly, and learn from past success.

Relate well to others

Self-discipline is fundamental to living a good, meaningful life. Making choices in life based purely on what we do and do not want to do will not get us very far. It would be chaos. If you study the lives of phenomenally successful people—from athletes to novelists to entrepreneurs—you will notice one consistent theme: self-discipline. Every day, regardless of the circumstances, they would do what is necessary to go ahead. They don't do it because they want to. They don't do it because it is convenient for them. They don't always do it after a nice night's sleep or because the mood strikes. They work hard every day, no matter what.

Destroy the opponents

You learn from the Navy SEALs that you have to accept competition. On the path to success, there will always be competition. Communicate well with your team and concentrate on reducing how to best counter it.

Everyday Tips

To remain on course, pay attention to the right cues

Determine which cues will help you maintain your self-control on a daily basis after answering the carrot or stick question. Having three hyper-productive days in a row has always been a challenge for me. I'll go two days without procrastinating, then on the third, the master procrastinator in my head takes control.

I usually leave visual cues on my desk at the end of my last productive day since I am more of a carrot person. If I have to complete an assignment, I'll leave out some of my previous work. This way, I'm happy to remind myself of the benefits of self-discipline.

In the same manner, I use clues that emphasize the link between short-term self-discipline and long-term achievement. Journal excerpts, for example, might indicate many hours of hard work right next to the paychecks that I received many months of hard work. Find methods to remind yourself of the power of everyday self-control, regardless of how you do it. The more reminders you have, the less likely you are to procrastinate and be lazy.

Accountability is a critical component of self-discipline

You must be responsible not just to others but also to yourself.

When it comes to personal responsibility, attempt to keep a journal of your journey and monitor your progress as often as possible. Write a few phrases in your journal every night if you want to improve your self-discipline. Include the good, the terrible, and the ugly of your current situation, and don't keep anything from yourself.

In the long term, you'll realize that self-mastery is nothing more than a collection of days in which you came closer to your objectives because of personal responsibility.

Aside from journaling, seeking assistance from your peers is also crucial. If you struggle with self-discipline, it helps to talk with someone who inspires you to stay the course, such as a spouse or a friend.

Final Words

It's been a long road through this book, and if you're still here, congrats on sticking with it. You've taken a few more steps down the hard road of self-discipline. We've looked at what self-discipline is, how it works, and how you can adapt it to benefit your life.

Those skills begin with changing your fundamental beliefs and self-beliefs like I also did many years ago. You need a mental image of the person you wish to be and reinforce it through smaller choices. For me, it began with morning rituals at university and progressed from there. I learned to chunk tasks, to work hard days with a lesser output if necessary, and to make daily schedules.

Since then, I've started to plan my life, regulate my thoughts and emotions, and promote my growth by adopting a better lifestyle that includes a healthy diet, exercise, relaxation, and socializing. Going beyond one's comfort zone in several aspects of life has also been beneficial. You may gain a lot from pushing your limits in general.

Most of us seek a moderate level of success, just enough to live our lives. It's about living a happy life, and most people don't want to be Elon Musk. They do not want to live to work. Most individuals want to enjoy themselves, which is just fine. I don't need billions to be happy.

Remember, this is a long-distance marathon, not a sprint. To be in it for the long haul, you must gradually adjust so as not to overburden yourself.

Exercise self-control and begin to break old, harmful behaviors. Again, take it gently if necessary. Don't overburden yourself. Your body and mind are key components of the machine that is you, and you need them to function efficiently in order to have the greatest chance of success.

Best wishes on your journey to self-discipline. I hope these strategies will help you. Now that you've reached this point, you're ready to start, so good luck!

***

If you enjoyed this book and the powerful tactics I provided inside, an honest review is always appreciated and will help us reach other listeners just like you who struggle with Self Discipline!

Good luck on your journey - Steve

References

- Duckworth, A. L. (2009). Self-discipline is empowering. Phi Delta Kappan, 90(7), 536.

- Duhigg, C. (2020). The Power of Habit. PTS Publishing House.

- Ford, L. R. (2007). 101 Ways to Improve Your Health. Lyall Ford.

- Gul, F., & Pesendorfer, W. (2001). Temptation and self-control. Econometrica, 69(6), 1403-1435.

- Jones, G., Hanton, S., & Connaughton, D. (2007). A framework of mental toughness in the world's best performers. The Sport Psychologist, 21(2), 243-264.

- Pashler, H. (2016). Attention. Psychology Press.

- Peters, P. S. (2020). Chimp paradox. Ebury Publishing.

- Rachman, Stanley J. Fear and courage. WH Freeman/Times Books/Henry Holt & Co, 1990.

- The Massachusetts Institute of Technology (MIT). Massachusetts Institute of Technology. (2021, December 26). Retrieved December 26, 2021, from https://www.mit.edu/

www.ingramcontent.com/pod-product-compliance
Lightning Source LLC
Chambersburg PA
CBHW071253070526
44583CB00017B/2450